AF372111

Bristol Impressions

Bristol Impressions

by Frank Shipsides

with text compiled by John Sansom

THE REDCLIFFE PRESS

First published in November 1977 by
Redcliffe Press Ltd., Bristol

First soft cover edition 1979
Second soft cover edition 1984

ISBN 0 905459 19 9

Printed in Great Britain by
Burleigh Ltd., Bristol

Contents

Illustrations

Preface

WE WERE naturally pleased when Frank Shipsides accepted our invitation to make this collection of pen-and-ink drawings of Bristol, as we believe that admirers of Mr. Shipsides' paintings will welcome an opportunity to see his draughtsmanship in book form.

There have been many excellent books about the city, but there is, we trust, a place for another, different view of Bristol—one seen through the keen eyes of the professional artist. Frank Shipsides' 'portrait' is sympathetically selective—he once said he couldn't paint an ugly building—but it nonetheless captures the special flavour that makes Bristol such a popular city.

In preparing the text to accompany Mr. Shipsides' drawings we have relied heavily on printed sources and on the assistance of the staff in the City Archivist's Department, Art Gallery and Public Relations Department all of whom, as always, have been exceptionally helpful. We must equally thank the staff of various organisations mentioned in the text, and also point out that references to particular buildings do not imply that they are necessarily open to the public.

In addition to the sources quoted on the following pages, we gratefully acknowledge our debt to the authors and books listed in the bibliography on page 83.

From the Lloyds Bank frieze

Around Corn Street

STAND AROUND the top end of Corn Street and, sooner or later, you'll
hear a Bristol resident explaining the origin of the expression 'paying on
the nail'. The four flat topped bronze pillars, or nails, outside the Corn
Exchange have thus given rise to one of Bristol's many pieces of harmless
mythology. Originally situated on the north side of All Saints' Church in
a closed walk called the Tolzey, they were moved the short distance to
their present site in 1771 and for many years were used by corn merchants
to show their samples and strike bargains. The first pillar near All Saints'
is the oldest and dates from the late Elizabethan era, as does the second
which was a gift to the city by Alderman Robert Kitchen, merchant and
mayor. The third pillar was made by Thomas Hobson of Bristol and
given by Nicholas Crisp of London in 1625 and the fourth was given in
1631 by George White, a Bristol merchant.

You are now at the centre of a remarkable group of buildings. The
Palladian-fronted Corn Exchange itself, built by John Wood the Elder
of Bath in 1743, sits comfortably in the newly created 'piazza' where
businessmen stroll, talking 'shop' and gossiping with colleagues, and
office staff hurry to their favourite sandwich bars. The corn trade still meet
here on Thursdays, but the great days of exchange are long since past.

Occasional trade shows and Friday's antiques and crafts market notwithstanding, the trading floor is sadly under-used these days. The Exchange was built originally around an open court, exposed to the weather, and merchants were quick to change their allegiance to the greater comfort of Charles Busby's Commercial Rooms which were completed nearby in 1811.

The Commercial Rooms are somewhat dwarfed by neighbouring buildings, and visitors on entering are surprised by the spaciousness of the Grand Coffee Room. This is one of the city's finest interiors. An outstanding feature is the lovely lantern light with twelve caryatides holding the saucer dome. An elegant wind vane, still in working order, served originally to indicate whether the wind was favourable for ships to sail up the Avon. The 'Rooms' were for many years a place where merchants and brokers met to make their bargains but they are now more than anything a businessmen's luncheon club. They are used occasionally for auctions, meetings and special functions. Many famous Bristolians have been associated with the Rooms and John McAdam, the roadbuilder, was the first president in 1811. The first telegraph office in Bristol was set up here in 1852.

Outside, the three statues represent the city, commerce and navigation, and the relief over the portico represents Britannia, with Neptune and Minerva, receiving tributes from the far corners of the earth.

One early November morning each year (the first, if it falls on a weekday) three morning-suited gentlemen can be observed arriving at the Commercial Rooms. These are the presidents of the Anchor, Dolphin

One of the bronze pillars which gave rise to the expression 'paying on the nail'

The Corn Exchange and All Saints' tower

Bristol Commercial Rooms where businessmen have met for over 150 years

and Grateful Societies founded in memory of Edward Colston the great philanthropist. They meet to exchange cheques to mark the start of a fortnight's fund raising in the period running up to Colston's birthday on November 13th. On that day, they meet again at the same place before proceeding to a joint commemoration service in All Saints' Church. Between them, the three societies collect upwards of £20,000 each year to help the elderly. Although non-partisan these days, the Anchor was originally Liberal; the Dolphin, first to be founded in 1749, appealed to Conservative sentiment in the city, and the Grateful was neutral.

Not far away, in St. Nicholas Street, stands the little known Stock Exchange building, in a heavy Italianate style with black marbled columns. Inside, are some fine tiles, art nouveau furnishings and some of

The Stock Exchange in St. Nicholas Street

the original seating used by brokers. Its function is now purely administrative but local stockbrokers and jobbers used to trade 'on the floor' until quite recently. The building was completed in 1903 at the personal expense of Sir George White, then president, and donated by him to the Exchange. The Bristol Stock Exchange was founded in 1845, and was for long recognized as the best market in the West of England, first in railway stocks and then in tramways, breweries and tobacco shares. It joined with the Birmingham, Cardiff, Swansea and Nottingham exchanges in 1966 to form the Midlands and Western Stock Exchange, later joined a federal system and now comes under the aegis of 'The Stock Exchange', a national body representing the London exchange and all regional exchanges with a common set of rules and laws.

Corn Street lies (as it has since banking proper started in earnest two centuries ago) at the heart of the city's financial and professional world. Few parts of Bristol have as great a sense of 'place' as the city: thronged with trade at lunchtime, or near deserted at six when the footfalls of late homegoers echo strangely down the empty streets. Corn Street's commercial buildings are largely Victorian, solid and respectable, their symbolism given an outward expression in the rich ornamentation of their façades. In complete contrast to the eighteenth century restraint of the Corn Exchange is the florid magnificence of Lloyds Bank, opposite at Number 55, Corn Street. Built in 1857, it is a spendid example of the revival of High Renaissance taste, its design by local architect W. B. Gingell in partnership with T. R. Lysaght being based on the Library of St. Mark's in Venice. It was commissioned by the West of England and South Wales District Bank which failed spectacularly in 1878, ruining most of its shareholders. Another local bank was formed and ran successfully until taken over by Lloyds towards the end of the century. The intricate frieze represents various commercial activities, with boys receiving, paying, storing and coining money and printing notes. Inside is an impressive and lofty banking hall, with an interesting little panel which gives the building's history and a detailed explanation of the symbolic sculpted figures on the exterior. On this site stood the Bush Inn, famous for its hospitality, and one of the city's major coaching inns. Edmund Burke campaigned here, and Charles Dickens had Mr. Winkle, in *Pickwick Papers* lodging here when searching for the missing Arabella Allen.

On the corner with Broad Street is Sir Robert Smirke's Old Council House. It was built in 1824 as offices for the Corporation and served as such until the growing demands of bureaucracy led to the building of the present Council House on College Green. This is one of those buildings one can pass daily and hardly notice. Its stark 'Greek Revival' exterior is appropriately topped by a figure of Justice (by Edward Baily, the Bristol sculptor)—for the Old Council House is now used by Bristol Crown Court. Half the world knows at least one example of Edward Baily's work, for he sculpted the Nelson figure on the Trafalgar Square column. Inside the Council House, a handsome staircase with brass and red composition inlay leads to a suite of fine rooms rarely seen by Bristolians, other than those of the criminal classes. The former Council Chamber is an exquisite little room, with gold leaf ceiling and paintings of royalty, and now serves as Crown Court Number 8. The Large Chamber, now Court Number 7 and the largest courtroom in Bristol, is another fine room with massive paintings commissioned earlier this century by local businessmen and donated to the city. Here are 'The chairing of Edmund Burke' by Frank Brangwyn; 'King Henry VII fining the citizens of Bristol because their wives so finely drest' by Tom Mostyn; 'The launch of the Great Western from Patterson's Yard, July 19th, 1837' by Wilde Parsons, and half a dozen more examples of the historical reconstructions which so delighted the Bristol public in the 1920s and 1930s. Court Number 6 contains portraits of former Lord Mayors and in the Judge's Room is a portrait of Colonel Adrian Scrope who was the last governor of Bristol Castle from 1649 to 1655 and who supervised its destruction under Cromwell. This room was the former Mayor's Parlour. Three bell pushes by the heavy Victorian fireplace are marked 'Treasurer', 'Town Clerk' and 'Housekeeper' respectively.

Opposite the Old Council House is All Saints' Church with its distinctive cupola tower. It is a perfect city church, accessible yet secret, and a sanctuary from the bustle of commerce outside. All Saints' dates from the early twelfth century but, like most churches of its antiquity, has evolved over the centuries. Much of the interior is fifteenth century, the long chancel was rebuilt in 1850 and the present tower, an exquisite Corn Street landmark, was completed in 1716. The most famous of its monuments is to Edward Colston and is backed by a tablet listing his many good works. The other end of Corn Street is dominated by the fine fifteenth century 'Somerset' tower of St. Stephen's, the city's parish church. The tower, surmounted by battlements and pinnacles, was erected at the expense of John Shipward, who was mayor several times. The church has interesting monuments, including one to Edmund Blanket, a wool merchant, and to Martin Pring who sailed to Cape Cod in 1603.

The porch of St. Stephen's, the city's parish church

Carwardines, coffee roasters and tea blenders since 1777, have a coffee shop ('the liquefaction of our torrefaction ensures satisfaction') next to All Saints', and on this site stood the London Coffee House of 1713.

Bristol's medieval High Cross, erected in 1373 to mark the granting of the royal charter, once stood at the junction of Broad Street, Corn Street, High Street and Wine Street. This spot now needs—and *has* needed ever since the Wine Street corner was lost in wartime bombing—something to replace the old cross and enclose the view from Corn Street. Bristol has the designers and makers who would surely respond to the challenge of creating a monument true to our own age but sympathetic to its historical context.

In Broad Street, the Christchurch we see today dates from the late 1780s. It is Bristol's finest church of the period. Its classical interior is all white and gold elegance with beautiful saucer domed ceilings supported on Corinthian columns. This is the work of William Paty, a family name which crops up regularly in books on Bristol's eighteenth century architecture. Paty's superb rood screen was originally designed as the reredos behind the altar but was replaced by the present stone reredos in 1882 when the church became the centre of the Tractarian Movement in Bristol. Happily, it was re-erected in 1928 as a rood screen and has been aptly described by Sir Nikolaus Pevsner as 'a light-hearted piece flanked by Louis XVI columns with a flower garland wound round'. There is a fine semi-circular altar rail made in wrought iron by Walter Swayne who was an iron-monger in Wine Street. Walter Ison, author of one of the two definitive books on Bristol's Georgian archi-tecture—the other is by C. F. W. Dening—points to similarities with St. Martin's-in-the-Fields but shows that its direct proto-type was Badminton Church in Gloucestershire.

The Christchurch quarter jacks, at which Robert Southey marvelled as a young boy

8

Outside, above the porch, is one of Bristol's best known curiosities—the carved quarterjack figures which strike the quarter hours. They are loaned to the church by Bristol corporation at a rent of 12½p a year. The poet Robert Southey, born in 1774 just round the corner in Wine Street, was baptised at Christchurch and as a young lad often stopped with his satchel on his back to see them strike. The jacks then adorned the old church which William Paty's design was soon to replace. They were not reinstated for some time, and Southey writing in 1806 could say 'my father had a great love for these poor quarter-boys, who had regulated all his movements for about twenty years; and when the church was rebuilt, offered to subscribe largely to their re-establishment. But the Wine streeters had no taste for the arts, and no feeling for old friends, and God knows what became of the poor fellows.'

Much of the delight of ancient cities lies in the variety of their street scenes. In Bristol, Orchard Street, home of Bristol Municipal Charities—and, it sometimes seems, of half the solicitors' practices in the city—retains its eighteenth century dignity. But Broad Street almost bursts with variety. The uses are as mixed as the buildings themselves—a major hotel, small retail shops, banks, building societies and insurance offices, steak bars, barristers' chambers, an old fashioned hairdressing saloon, offices for the Open University, a cellar pub (Bristol is full of subterranean bars and restaurants), law courts and a church at either end.

The well named Grand Hotel has ministered to the needs of travellers since 1869, but it was not the first hotel on the site. Sir Thomas Lawrence's father was landlord of the White Lion when it was an important picking up point for the daily mail coaches to London, the West and the Midlands.

On the corner of Broad Street and John Street is a pleasant surprise, an office development which in many ways is a textbook example of 'good neighbourly' design. The developers, their architects and the city's planning committee can all take immense credit for a thoughtful scheme which respects the scale of its surroundings, preserves a number of important buildings and creates a strikingly attractive modern office block into the bargain. The visual highlight of the scheme is the fantastic Edward Everard frontage. Everard owned a printing works and when, in 1900, the Broad Street premises were being planned, he commissioned W. J. Neatby of the Doulton Company to design a highly decorated

Broad Street looking towards St. John's Gate

facade using Carrara marble ware tiles. Everard's inspiration was medieval art and the current arts and crafts revival led by William Morris. In *A Bristol Printing House*, he explains how these influences shaped his remarkable tribute to the masters of the printer's art. The design is surmounted by a symbol of Light and Truth holding a lamp and mirror; below, a winged figure representing the Spirit of Literature is flanked on one side by Gutenberg at his printing press and on the other by William Morris similarly employed. A magnificent Art Nouveau gate in wrought iron now leads to offices of the National Westminster Bank where visitors can see an interesting little collection of art nouveau items.

The Queen's Silver Jubilee visit on August 8th, 1977 must have set some minds wondering how much of old Bristol the first Queen Elizabeth would recognize today. Her complimentary remarks about St. Mary Redcliffe when she visited the city in 1574 are well known, and St. John's Arch, at the bottom of Broad Street would not be unfamiliar, despite the soaring office blocks which now surround it. This is the only surviving medieval city gate and the tiny church of St. John's is built onto the original wall. Elizabeth passed through this arch, to be addressed by boys representing Salutation, Gratulation and Obedient Goodwill.

The church interior is simply designed and decorated; much of the furnishing is Jacobean, and an unusual little curiosity is an eighteenth century pulpit hour-glass. The Reverend George Whitefield, the great Methodist pioneer, preached his first Bristol sermon here in 1737. He was in great demand, and invited to several churches in the city, including St. Stephen's and The Mayor's Chapel. He sometimes preached four times a day, often to overflowing churches, before sailing to Georgia.

The statues above the arch on the Broad Street side are said to represent Brennus and Belinus, the mythical founders of the city. In Nelson Street, in the north wall of the church, is a water conduit which has flowed for almost six hundred years from a spring at the top of Park Street. The spring belonged to Carmelite Friars who ran the water down the hill through Frog Lane and along Pipe Lane to a cistern at the nearby friary. From there, they granted a 'feather' pipe to the vestry of St. John's. Parishioners used to collect the water for their domestic use. A plaque by the conduit records that, for a short time during the war years, this was the only water supply to the blitzed centre of the city.

*Seventeenth century houses
in King Street*

King Street

IF AN American friend had just ten minutes to see just one Bristol thorough-fare, it would be difficult to know which to suggest. Broad Street, Corn Street, King Street, Queen Square, St. Michael's Hill are all equally distinguished in their different ways. But rephrase the question and ask which street could Bristol least afford to lose? It then perhaps is King Street for its overall variety of architectural styles and the outstanding interest and quality of its individual buildings. Few streets can boast such variety in the space of a couple of hundred yards: the oldest working theatre in the country, a magnificent former guild hall, two groups of almshouses, gabled seventeenth century houses, an early municipal library where Coleridge and Southey read, imposing Victorian warehouses and a romantic half-timbered inn oozing with historical associations.

King Street was laid out in the mid-seventeenth century, a remarkably wide thoroughfare for its time, and the St. Nicholas almshouses and other original houses survive from those days. The street's greatest jewel is the Theatre Royal, which now incorporates the Palladian-fronted Coopers' Hall designed by William Halfpenny. The theatre opened its doors to the rich merchant families then living in King Street and nearby

*The Theatre Royal, Coopers' Hall
and St. Nicholas' almshouses with the
Robinson Building in the background*

Queen Square on May 31st, 1766. David Garrick, the celebrated actor, strangely never performed here (almost every famous name since has done so) but he wrote the prologue to Steel's *The Conscious Lovers* with which the theatre opened, and described the new theatre as the most beautiful in Europe. The opening night had to be billed as 'a concert of music interspersed with specimens of rhetorick' to circumvent the law. The Puritans had failed to prevent the theatre being built but, at least initially, had succeeded in denying a licence to perform plays.

The Theatre Royal flourished for many years, only to be eclipsed during the nineteenth century by a new theatre, later to be called the Prince's, on Park Row. Its decline was hastened by the social decline of the docks area around King Street. The grand old theatre was reduced to performing third rate variety to audiences which would have horrified the gentry who flocked there in its heyday. Its lowest ebb had been reached by the early 1940s when, on the verge of being turned into a warehouse, it was bought by public spirited citizens and leased to the forerunner of today's Arts Council, which sponsored its wartime productions. After the war, the Bristol Old Vic Company was established and by the time of the theatre's bi-centenary celebrations in 1966, plans were being drawn up for the next leap forward. An ambitious restoration scheme embraced the Coopers' Hall (providing a more impressive entrance), improved backstage facilities and a new experimental theatre. Another crisis loomed when the generous financial support from local and national sources proved inadequate in the face of inflating costs. The Bristol & West Building Society bridged the gap with a substantial loan and the Theatre Royal enjoyed a glittering re-opening, in January 1972, with Hayley Mills and Ian Richardson in the première of *Trelawny*, a highly successful musical.

In lower key, the almshouses bring a note of serenity to a street which is being slowly engulfed by newly fashioned 'olde worlde' pubs. The eight-gabled St. Nicholas almshouses stand between the Coopers' Hall and Queen Charlotte Street. They were built in 1652 and supported for many years by St. Peter's Hospital. Now administered by the Society of Merchant Venturers, they provide

One of Bristol's finest shell hood doorways

charming homes for ten elderly ladies. A fragment of the old city wall was discovered during building work twenty years ago. The Society also run the pretty pink coloured Merchants' almshouses, next to the Old Library, at the western end of the street. The building dates from 1696, but the almshouses were founded for retired sailors much earlier and have been in the Merchant Venturers' care almost since time immemorial.

The present almshouses originally stood four sided around a quadrangle, but one wing was lost to enemy bombs, which also destroyed the adjoining Merchants' Hall. Generations of 'old salts' have ended their days here, swopping yarns about their seafaring exploits. An Edgar Allan Poe story, the *Gold Beetle*, is said to be based on the published memoirs of one old resident. On the seaman's death a manuscript account of his adventures, *The Journal of Llewellin Penrose, a Seaman*, came to light and publication was arranged with illustrations by Bristol artists.

A board fixed to the almshouses bears a charming poem, in gilt letters, which reads—

> *Freed from all storms, the tempest, and the rage*
> > *Of billows, here we spend our age;*
> *Our weather-beaten vessels here repair,—*
> *And from the Merchants' kind and generous care,*
> *Find harbour here; no more we put to sea*
> > *Until we launch into Eternity.*
> *And lest our widows whom we leave behind,*
> *Should want relief, they too a shelter find;*
> *Thus all our anxious cares and sorrows cease,*
> *Whilst our kind Guardians turn our toils to ease;*
> *May they be with an endless Sabbath blest,*
> *Who have afforded unto us this rest.*

The destruction of the magnificent Merchants' Hall was a terrible loss. After prolonged soul searching, the Society decided not to rebuild on the King Street corner it had occupied since its foundation four hundred years earlier, and instead moved its headquarters to The Promenade, Clifton. And so central Bristol lost a historic link with an organisation which once exercised immense commercial influence in the city. The Society received its royal charter from Edward VI in 1552 and for centuries it represented the interests of the powerful merchant classes, controlled the port, and was an important land owner. From the early days, though, the Society was involved in the charitable and educational work which were to blossom as its economic power declined in later years. It still plays an important role in these fields, in its own right and as trustee for a number of charitable trusts.

The half-timbered Llandoger Trow is Bristol's finest old inn. Its gabled black and white front epitomises most people's ideal of an ancient pub, and has the virtue of being authentic. The inn's unusual name is taken from the Severn trows, small sailing ships which used to ply between Llandogo in the Wye Valley and the Welsh Back quays just a stone's throw from the inn. Bristol mythology insists that Robert Louis Stevenson's 'Spyglass Inn' in *Treasure Island* was modelled on it. Inside, among the low ceilings, seventeenth century plasterwork, panelling and staircases, it is not difficult to romanticise about rum swigging pirates, Long John Silver and all. A more likely model, though, was the old Coach and Horses, on The Grove, and perhaps now incorporated into The Hole in the Wall. But the Llandoger Trow is one of the inns at which Daniel Defoe might well have met the real life Alexander Selkirk who became the fictional Robinson Crusoe. For Captain Woodes Rogers, one of Bristol's most successful sailors, lived nearby in Queen Square and seems certain to have frequented his local inn. And it was he who found Selkirk the castaway on the Island of Juan Fernandez and brought him back to Bristol. There are other colourful associations. The inn is full of old playbills, a reminder of its long association with visiting actors and actresses—Henry Irving, Kate Terry and Beerbohm Tree were regulars. Opposite the Llandoger Trow is the Old Duke, a popular jazz club with a hanging sign depicting Duke Ellington which was painted by Peter Harrison, a local artist, in 1974. Not far away, the Bunch of Grapes is one of those friendly and unspoilt little pubs of which Bristol now has so few.

The Llandoger Trow, a popular Bristol inn since 1664

St. Thomas' Church behind a group of
seventeenth century houses

The city skyline behind Bristol Bridge

Bristol Bridge

LOOKING BACK to his Edwardian youth, Compton Mackenzie once wrote a charming essay on the vanished colours and smells of London town. It could be true that Bristol, too, lost some of its distinctive aromas when the great merchant ships stopped bringing their cargoes of sherry, tobacco, and bananas right into the heart of the city. But at Bristol Bridge the morning smell of malted barley being mashed still curls down Baldwin Street when the wind is from the east. Beer has been brewed here alongside the river for centuries. In 1788, Philip George and six other Bristol merchants bought the brewery which bore his family name until 1961 when it was taken over by the Courage group. Half a million barrels (each holding thirty-six gallons) of beer a year are now produced at the Bristol brewery. That's a staggering 144,000,000 pints. Courage also brew special beers here, like the Promotion Ale brewed in 1976 to mark Bristol City's return to Division One of the Football League.

Bristol Bridge is reckoned to have inspired the city's name. Scholars differ about its precise origin, but the popular explanation is that it derives from the Saxon *Brigstow* (the place of the bridge). Today, Bristol may have no obvious focal point, but for centuries it lay here, stretching from the river through the ancient, tight-packed shopping streets covering what is now the Castle Green. The shops were flattened by enemy night raids in the terrible November of 1940, a new shopping centre was built after the war in nearby Broadmead, and Sir Hugh Casson was commissioned to oversee the refashioning of the old site. Various ambitious plans were mooted to make something very special of a part of the city dear to Bristolian hearts. In the event, mounting costs and civic timidity resulted in Bristol settling for a partial reconstruction of the long lost castle walls, the restoration of two small vaulted rooms uncovered by war damage, and the retention of the remains of St. Mary-le-port and St. Peter's churches. The rest of the area has been grassed over and a number of trees planted—all pleasant enough with a riverside walk, but, many local people feel, failing to do justice to the site.

From the ruins of St. Peter's is a good view of the city skyline with its churches still very much in evidence and the medieval tower of St. Mary-le-port in the foreground. A tablet in the south wall of St. Peter's marks the burial place of Richard Savage, a disreputable poet friend of Samuel Johnson's. He died in Newgate Jail in 1743 and is commemorated by a plaque at Fairfax House, on the corner of Union Street and Newgate. Francis Greenway, the architect, was imprisoned here in 1812. Greenway designed the Assembly Rooms (now the Clifton Club) in The Mall, Clifton and worked on various Clifton houses. A dispute over one of these led to his being found guilty at Bristol Assizes of forging a £250 promissory note and transported for life to Australia. There his fortunes recovered, he designed the Australian Houses of Parliament and became known as the father of Australian architecture. On August 1st, 1977, Mr. Gordon Freeth, the Australian High Commissioner, unveiled a plaque at the Clifton Club to commemorate the 200th anniversary of the architect's birth.

Visitors to Bristol Bridge may observe the church clock with the second hand. In this, St. Nicholas is said to be unique in this country, but a much greater cause for wonder is the ecclesiastical museum now housed in the church. It contains a splendid collection of silver and other church plate from local churches, relics and old photographs illustrating the growth of the city and watercolour drawings from the much prized Braikenridge collection. George Weare Braikenridge was an antiquarian and retired

*The Shakespeare Inn and the
leaning tower of Temple Church*

merchant who had owned plantations in the West Indies. In the days before photography, he commissioned local artists to draw Bristol scenes. The result was nearly 1,500 drawings completed between 1818 and 1830, now owned by the City Art Gallery, and which give us a remarkable insight into what Bristol looked like then. Some of the Braikenridge artists, notably T. L. S. Rowbotham, are included in *The Bristol Scene*, a booklet compiled by the Art Gallery.

The delicate wash of the Braikenridge artists contrasts nicely with the group of large oil paintings which the church museum also houses. Far and away the most important of these is the magnificent Hogarth tryptych which originally adorned St. Mary Redcliffe. This masterpiece in the grand scale is itself quite out of keeping with the satirically observed scenes from contemporary society for which Hogarth is so well known. The artist's only other work on this scale were two large Biblical paintings for the Hospital of St. Bartholomew in London in 1735-36.

The present St. Nicholas, its interior rebuilt to a simplified plan after being gutted in the Second World War, dates from the 1760s. Its predecessor had stood over one of the town gates and the original crypt survives to this day. On November 14th the girls of Red Maids' School celebrate Whitson's Day at a special service in the crypt. They are honouring Alderman John Whitson whose will provided for the foundation of a school for the maintenance and training of forty girls, daughters of burgesses, 'to go and be apparelled in red cloth'. The school opened in 1634, and the girls have worn the distinctive red clothes, with white fichu, apron and bonnet, ever since. At the service, the head girls place wreaths on their benefactor's tomb. The Red Maids may continue to wear the traditional garb decreed by Whitson, but one curious feature from the early days has long since gone—the girls are no longer served half a pint of beer at breakfast, dinner and supper!

John Whitson, once described as Bristol's Dick Whittington, led a most interesting life. Born in the Forest of Dean, he came to Bristol as a lad, and was apprenticed in 1570 to Nicholas Cutt, a local mercer. When his master died ten years later, Whitson astutely married his widow (by then a wealthy woman), became the most influential merchant of his day served twice as Mayor and five times as member of Parliament. He died in 1629 at the age of seventy-five when the horse he was riding

Bristol's colourful Flower Market

- FRANK SHIPSIDES - 1977 -

stumbled and fell. His funeral was marked with great ceremony, and the list of funeral expenses makes bizarre reading to the modern eye: 'Epitaph, 10s; Mustard, 1d; Making 75 gowns for the poor, 75s; Wine from the Bull, £5 17s 6d; Making a coffin, 14s; Baking of pies, 7s 6d; To Mr. Palmer for making the verses on the monument, 20s.'

At the west end of the church, steps run up from Baldwin Street to the colourful Flower Market in St. Nicholas Street. This was the wholesale fruit and vegetable market, too, until transport problems forced a move, in 1968, to a new one million pound market at St. Philips. A miscellany of stall-holders sell anything from afghan raisins to dog-eared paperbacks. The general standard of the stalls is low, however, and anyone expecting a Caledonian Market or a Brighton Lanes atmosphere will be disappointed by the strange 'flatness' of the scene—but it *is* a good place to buy flowers, drink a glass of Bristol Milk sherry or tuck into a Berni steak. For here are the cellar bars for which Bristol is renowned—'large glass, sir, or schooner?'—and here, too, is the venerable Rummer Inn. There have been inns on this site since 1241. Many notables are said to have stayed here including Oliver Cromwell, and the Rummer was once one of the three principal coaching inns in the city. The first mail coach trip from London to Bristol arrived at the Rummer's High Street entrance in August, 1784 after a fifteen hour journey. In the nineteenth century the inn was a stronghold of pugilism and served as the headquarters of several well known patrons of the sport. For a while, Coleridge published *The Watchman* periodical from here, but it folded after ten issues with Joseph Cottle, Coleridge's bookseller-cum-publisher friend bearing most of the loss. Inside, are a large 'rummer' drinking vessel in beaten copper which was probably once an inn sign, and an Act of Parliament clock, so named because these public clocks were introduced when an Act of 1797 taxed clocks and watches with the result that people just stopped carrying watches. The Rummer was acquired by the Berni brothers about twenty years ago to become the first West Country steak bar, starting quite a social revolution. Bernis alone now have one hundred and fifty-one steak bars throughout the country.

From Bristol Bridge there are fine views down the water, with Redcliffe Parade in the far distance, the Robinson Building dominating the foreground to the left and the cobbled Welsh Back, with its Bristol

Byzantine warehouse to the right. The attractive row of plane trees skirting the quayside were provided by Bristol Civic Society's 'Trees-for-Bristol-streets' scheme. Over four hundred trees have been planted since this was launched in 1973. The Civic Society raises the cash from individuals and businesses (the donor's name can be displayed on the tree) and the City's parks department looks after the planting and maintenance. It's an inspired partnership, and other cities might well consider emulating such an imaginative scheme.

Victoria Street runs south from Bristol Bridge. It was once known as the Ugliest Street in Europe. Most of its Victorian buildings have now gone, victims of the bombs and demolition gangs, and what remains is dispiriting to a degree. Whatever its supposed architectural faults, the old Victoria Street had style and a sense of purpose marvellously caught in the cover photograph of Reece Winstone's *Bristol in the 1880s*, with Robinson's Dome and, in the foreground, a curly brimmed bowler-hatted gentleman striding confidently across the bridge. The scene today is one of empty office blocks no one seems to want, waste sites turned into car parks and decayed houses awaiting demolition. And thousands of young families would like a home of their own!

The new Robinson Building, at Number One, Redcliffe Street, aroused intense controversy when it hit the city skyline in 1964. It was Bristol's first tower block, voted by one engineering magazine as the third ugliest building in the country and described by Ian Nairn as one of only a dozen new buildings in the country worth a visit. Even today, people either love the Robinson Building or hate it. Despite its size, the building is remarkably sympathetic to its water-side setting and, in Bristol, has few rivals for its elegance of line and simplicity of detail.

Nearby, at the junction of Victoria Street and St. Thomas' Street, is an attractive group of gabled houses dating from 1673. They adjoin one of the city's least known churches—the Georgian church of St. Thomas the Martyr which retains an earlier medieval tower. Its somewhat forbidding exterior belies the quiet beauty of its tunnel-vaulted interior. There is a fine organ, dating from 1730, on which Handel is reputed to have composed part of his *Judas Maccabeus*. The church has long been renowned for its treasures: an illuminated folio manuscript Vulgate, valuable Georgian altar-plate and four champlevé enamelled thirteenth century candlesticks

Newly planted trees around the shell of St. Peter's Church

which can now be seen in the St. Nicholas Church Museum. St. Thomas is one of the six city churches which may be declared redundant (that is, no longer to be used for public worship). Each of the churches is too precious to be demolished, and alternative uses are being sought; St. Thomas, with its fine musical tradition, would make an admirable little concert hall.

Further along Victoria Street, on the left, stands the Shakespeare Inn of 1636, with a fine half-timbered front. Tenuous links have been claimed with the great playwright (although he died twenty years earlier), and legend has it that Dick Turpin frequented the bar parlour. There are other old pubs in the area: The Seven Stars, where Thomas Clarkson collected evidence about Bristol's slave traffic; the Cornubia in Temple Street which once boasted at least eighteen inns; and also in the vicinity there is a delightful little pub, with its Victorian interior largely unchanged, and which is best left unpublicised.

Temple Church is Bristol's modest answer to the leaning tower of Pisa. It was gutted by enemy bombs, but the 114 foot tower, leaning five feet out of true, was already a tourist attraction centuries ago. The Temple district takes its name from the Knights Templars who were granted land here in the twelfth century. It was for many years the centre of Bristol's weaving community. Edward Colston was born and christened here in 1636 and John Wesley preached in the church in the 1780s. The church exterior has been made safe by the Department of the Environment and the ruins are now open to visitors. With the adjoining Temple Gardens, this is a delightful little backwater tucked in beneath the new office blocks to the north and east. Will the future redevelopment of the remaining area respect the special, narrow-laned atmosphere of ancient Temple?

The Stag & Hounds,
where the pie poudre court was
held for many years

Old Market

The church of St. Philip and St. Jacob

UNTIL 1971, an interesting little ceremony could be observed outside the 'Stag and Hounds' in Old Market Street on September 30th each year. The opening and closing proclamations of the ancient Pie Poudre Court were read, with due solemnity, even though the court had long since ceased to have any practical significance. The Crown Courts Act of 1970 swept away this harmless anachronism which had its origins in the need for summary, on-the-spot justice to settle disputes arising from the annual fairs held in Old Market. In medieval times there were three pie poudre or 'dusty feet' courts in Bristol, the oldest charter being granted in 1170 to the Prior of St. James.

The eminent historian, John Latimer tells in *The Annals of Bristol* how, in 1836, Sir Charles Wetherell as Recorder decided to conduct the Pie Poudre proceedings strictly according to the ancient custom. Toast, cheese and mead were provided for the official staff and friends, with beer and cider for the commonalty. Despite the drunken scenes which followed Sir Charles Wetherell kept strictly to the book. The summoning of a long roll of people 'to come forth and do suit and service'—although they had been dead for centuries—was another farce of this ancient tribunal; but Sir Charles never relaxed a muscle when, in replying to the clerk, he declined to fine the defaulters for non-attendance, seeing that, as he was informed, they could not be found. The yearly disturbance arising from the feast ultimately led to its suppression, and the proceedings were immediately adjourned to another court after the customary opening ceremony. But now even this simple ritual has been dispensed with, and with it a little bit of old Bristol has slipped away for ever.

The Stag and Hounds is an interesting old inn with columns supporting the first floor and forming a covered way over the pavement—a feature also to be seen at the eighteenth century Kingsley Hall nearby. Like other public houses in the area, it has so far escaped the full horror of modernisation. The Palace Hotel, still advertising Ushers Noted 6d Beers on its façade, retains something of its Victorian interior, with attractive glass and barley-sugar pillars.

Old Market Street is not a part of Bristol that finds its way into the guidebooks; falling apart, an odd mixture of shops, industry, commerce and old people's housing, it lies at the mercy of the planners and developers. It is one of the city's ancient thoroughfares, once the main road to London and an important centre of trade. Its name speaks for itself, and the Castle market was held here for centuries. Here is a wealth of minor architectural detail, gabled houses and pantiled roofs, Georgian shops— a wonderful jumble of a place, once vigorous and full of character, that cries out for a new lease of life.

Even now, the street has pleasant surprises for the inquisitive. For here, a little oasis of peace among the traffic's roar, are the Trinity South Almshouses. The present buildings, around a pleasant lawn, date from 1858 and were designed by local architects, Foster and Wood. Despite the different styles—the Trinity buildings are 'Tudor'—it's not hard to see that the same hand also designed Foster's Almshouses on Christmas Steps. The Trinity almshouses were founded in 1402 by John Barstaple, a Bristol businessman who was three times Mayor. The chapel was the last resting place for the benefactor and his wife Isabella whose burials are marked with engraved brasses. Across the other side of Old Market Street are other almshouses, too.

Redcross Street, built as a by-pass for traffic on market days, runs parallel to Old Market Street on its north side. It holds little interest, but Sir Thomas Lawrence, Royal portrait painter to George III, was born at number six. In a curious Bristol fashion, the house *next door* was preserved when the painter's birthplace was demolished for a new office block. Lawrence was born here in 1769, the youngest of sixteen children. He started young, making crayon drawings of guests at his father's inn when

On the south side of Old Market Street are the little known Trinity South almshouses

31

he was five years old. Bristol possesses a few portraits, including those of The Duke of Portland and Lady Caroline Lamb, but apart from the accident of birth, Lawrence's story lies not in Bristol but in the wealthy houses of fashionable London in the late eighteenth and early nineteenth centuries.

To the south, lie interesting old warehouses, seedy back streets, derelict sites and Broad Plain, with a row of superb eighteenth century houses. On the Old Market Roundabout, the *Evening Post* and *Western Daily Press* have settled into their new, purple-bricked headquarters. This is a building of rare panache which received a RIBA commendation in 1975. Across Temple Way, amid surprising greenery, is the church of St. Philip and St. Jacob. Its congregation is one of the liveliest in Bristol, dedicated to social work and illustrating in the most positive way that the church has a vital role to play in modern society.

The strange tower rising from the waterside by Cheese Lane is used for the manufacture of lead shot. The technique of pouring molten lead through small holes into water has hardly changed since the process was invented by William Watts, a Redcliffe plumber, in 1782. There is a delightful story about how he came to make his remarkable discovery. Legend has it that Watts (or his wife, it hardly matters which) dreamed of seeing molten lead being poured from a great height, assuming small spherical shapes as it fell into a bucket of water. Experiments the following morning convinced Watts that the idea would work, he obtained a patent for the process and extended the height of his Redcliffe Hill house, and was soon in business as a patent shot manufacturer. He quickly amassed a fortune which he even more quickly lost in a speculative building enterprise in Windsor Terrace, Clifton. His business was taken over in 1794 and the process was continued at the well-loved tower on Redcliffe Hill until it was demolished for road widening only nine years ago. The Sheldon Bush & Patent Shot Company then commissioned a local firm of structural engineers to design the new 141-foot tower in Cheese Lane. The Y-shaped shaft is a good example of how a building's use determines its outward shape, being designed to meet three requirements: a 120-foot lead drop, a staircase and a hoist. In 1969 the tower won a Civic Trust award.

The Sheldon Bush shot tower, a notable waterside landmark

*Chatterton's birthplace in
Redcliffe Way*

Redcliffe

BRISTOL'S MOST widely celebrated building is St. Mary Redcliffe church. Most guidebooks recall that in 1574 Queen Elizabeth I dubbed it 'the fairest, goodliest and most famous parish church in England' and visitors can be forgiven for assuming that *this* is Bristol's cathedral. The boy poet Thomas Chatterton wrote that it was 'the pride of Brigstowe and the western land'.

No visitor to Bristol, no matter how rushed or worldly wise, should think of leaving the city without indulging the sense of wonder and humility which this beautiful church never fails to invoke. Its magnificent exterior, its flying buttresses, pinnacles and soaring spire, its superb north porch, are matched by the splendour of its interior, with its slender columns soaring in uninterrupted majesty, its 1,220 roof bosses covered with pure gold, its beautifully vaulted transepts, its great windows and its rare relics—relics not of saints but of Bristol's great merchant venturers

St. Mary Redcliffe's name is indelibly written in the city's long history. John and Sebastian Cabot lived in nearby Cathay, and are depicted in the great south transept window. Quite possibly Richard Amerike, Sheriff at the time of their return to Bristol after discovering Newfoundland was the source of the new continent's name rather than the Italian Amerigo Vespucci. Those were the days when Redcliffe could boast an identity quite separate from that of Bristol's. Wealthy merchants built great houses here; their ships sailed the high seas earning the fortunes which helped create this beautiful church.

In the fifteenth century, William Canynges the younger, wealthy merchant and benefactor, was mayor of Bristol no fewer than five times and its Member of Parliament twice. He owned a larger fleet of ships than any other Bristol merchant in the fifteenth century, and had ten vessels totalling 2,500 tons—tiny vessels by our standards, but large enough to create a massive fortune for their owner. Canynges' name is inextricably linked with that of St. Mary Redcliffe. He financed restoration on a massive scale and founded two chantries and, after his wife's death, he entered the church fully to be ordained in 1468. Canynges' magnificent tomb shows the wealthy merchant and his wife in splendid costume, while another effigy depicts Canynges the priest in more suitably simple dress. Another famous Redcliffe name is that of the Penn family. Admiral Sir William Penn, born in 1621, fought in the Dutch wars and was knighted for his naval exploits. He is buried at the entrance to the south transept, and his armour can be seen above an epitaph at the west end of the church. His son, also William, established a Quaker colony in America and gave his family name to the state of Pennsylvania. William Hogarth painted his great tryptych altarpiece for St. Mary Redcliffe in 1755. The three panels, representing *The Ascension of Christ*, *The Sealing of the Sepulchre*, and *The Three Marys at the Tomb* are now housed in the St. Nicholas Church Museum in Baldwin Street. Handel was a friend of Thomas Broughton, then vicar, and revised some of his oratories on the church organ. The Handel window, in which are scored eight passages from *The Messiah*, commemorates the great composer's links with the church. Poets Coleridge and Southey were married to the Fricker sisters at St. Mary Redcliffe in 1795.

St. Mary Redcliffe has its share of ancient city customs. At Whitsun,

St. Mary Redcliffe Church seen across the water from The Welsh Back

36

during the Rush Sunday ceremony, green rushes are scattered on the floor of the church. The ceremony is in remembrance of William Canynges' ordination as a priest, dates from 1493 and is attended by city dignitaries carrying the traditional posies of flowers. In September, the Redcliffe Pipe Walk commemorates an ancient easement, dating from 1190 when Sir Robert de Berkeley allowed water to be piped across his land from Knowle through Bedminster to the church. The underground course of the water is marked by fourteen stones. The vicar, church-wardens and parishioners walk the course annually and at each stone a member of the party is 'bumped'. A bronze tablet commemorating Sir Robert's unusual gift can be seen by the pool below the balustraded walk to the west of the church. A lovely ceremony (but by no means unique to St. Mary Redcliffe) takes places at Christmas when, at the Christingle children's service, each child is given an orange with candle and small fruits. The orange represents the world, the candle is Jesus Christ, light of the world, and the fruits are the fruits of the earth.

The church's magnificent north porch, with its strangely oriental outer doorway, looks onto as bleak a setting as one could imagine—a contrast of beauty and dereliction often seen in modern Bristol. Happily, the churchyard to the south, with its avenues of lime trees and bounded by the eighteenth century houses of Colston Parade, has a more appropriate serenity. Here is Fry's House of Mercy, endowed by William Fry, a distiller, in 1784. Fry drew up the house rules. The almswomen, he decreed, should be well-bred, moral and religious; vicious persons and drunkards would not be admitted, and there would be a sixpenny fine for failure to attend church services.

At number 9, Colston Parade a plaque marks the birthplace of Samuel Plimsoll who became famous as the 'sailor's friend'. After early careers in a solicitor's office and in a brewery, he was elected MP for Derby in 1868. He then campaigned for a compulsory load line on ships to protect sailors from the dangers of overloaded cargoes. The Merchant Shipping Act of 1876 and the introduction of the Plimsoll Line were the outcome. Plimsoll is also commemorated by a bust on the water's edge at Hotwells.

Glass-making was once a great local industry—the characteristic blue and green 'Bristol glass' is world famous—and Redcliffe was an import-ant centre of manufacture. In 1725, Alexander Pope was able to write,

*Bathurst Basin looking towards the
Ostrich Inn and Redcliffe Parade*

somewhat inelegantly, that Bristol had 'no less than fifteen glass houses, which is more than in London' and old views of the city show the furnace 'cones' sticking up like sore thumbs among the surrounding houses. One Redcliffe kiln survives, in Prewett Street, restored and converted into a restaurant in the Dragonara Hotel.

Guinea Street houses

Across Redcliffe Hill from the church lies one of Bristol's most pleasing modern buildings, housing the Administration Centre of the Phoenix Assurance Company. An attractive enclosed square, echoing the Georgian style, fronts on to Guinea Street. Here is a notable survival from 1718—a group of three houses (originally the home of Captain Edmund Saunders) with an unusual gable and picturesque carvings above each window. It's a short walk here to the waterfront. Nearby is dignified Redcliffe Parade, its houses mostly converted into offices with fine views over the Floating Harbour and the city. Below are labyrinthine caves, cut out of the sandstone cliffs which give the district its name. The caves can occasionally be visited and guides will discourse on the mystery surrounding their origins—were they excavated for glass and pottery, used by smugglers or as storage by wine shippers? It's all innocent speculation, even if no one now believes they once housed negro slaves!

Of Bristol's many literary associations, none stirs the imagination more than the story of Thomas Chatterton. He was born on November 20th, 1752, son of a charity school master and his modest birthplace in Redcliffe Way can be visited at certain times. It houses a small Chatterton museum. The young poet's father had died by the time he was born and a culturally deprived background, frustrated ambition and a soaring romanticism, combined to produce the famous Rowley 'forgeries'.

Chatterton had achieved a modest literary success by the age of ten but there was nobody at that critical stage to encourage and channel his precocious talents. He was attracted by the Gothic splendour and antiquities of his parish church and spent many hours in the muniment room there studying old manuscripts which were quite clearly an inspiration for his 'medieval' poems. Leaving Colston School, where he found the commercial emphasis stifling, he became articled to a lawyer in Corn Street. In his spare time, Chatterton wrote the mock medieval poems which he attributed to Thomas Rowley, a fictitious fifteenth century priest. These were well enough done to fool the public initially and the controversy about their authenticity continued after the young poet's death. In 1776 Samuel Johnson, accompanied by the faithful Boswell, was persuaded to make a special visit to the muniment room. By then the 'marvellous boy, the sleepless soul that perished in his pride', in Wordsworth's lines, had been dead six years. Chatterton was sacked when John Lambert, his Corn Street employer, discovered a maliciously worded 'will'. He left for London, bitter at his lack of true recognition, worked furiously for a while but finally committed suicide in a Holborn garret in August 1770. He was seventeen years old.

To young poets Chatterton became, in today's language, a 'cult figure' and something of an inspiration to the burgeoning Romantic Movement. The quality of his astonishing output—by no means limited to the forgeries and in print running to over 600 pages—was uneven but remarkably mature for someone so young. Dr. Basil Cottle has shown that, with all their faults of construction and language, the Rowley poems contain passages of great beauty and inventiveness.

Dock cottages and small craft at Cumberland Basin

On the Waterfront

THE BEST time to visit Bristol's city docks extending from Neptune's statue on the Centre is during the annual Water Festival. For then the derelict quays bustle with people in and around boats—a bewildering variety of pleasure craft, the occasional venerable sailing barge brought in by its proud owners, and foreign warships on goodwill missions. It's a colourful spectacle, with the forest of masts a reminder of the city's past and a pointer, one hopes, to the time when life returns permanently to the dockland area. Seafaring was for centuries the central fact of Bristol life. Even now the city's special atmosphere owes much to its historical associations with the sea. Cabot, the wine trade, tobacco, privateering, Isambard Kingdom Brunel...Bristol is rich in everyday reminders of the past.

The city docks, encompassed within the nineteenth century Floating Harbour, have been overshadowed for many years by Avonmouth docks, but they were still handling over one million tons of cargo annually in the mid-1960s and only a few years ago Russian and Scandinavian ships could be seen moored alongside St. Augustine's Reach. But the decline

41

has accelerated and sandhoppers and occasional timber ships are now virtually the only commercial traffic using the Floating Harbour.

The water used to reach right up the Centre to what is now Electricity House. This stretch was partially culverted and decked over in the 1890s and completed in the late 1930s. Travel writer H. V. Morton was still able to muse, between the wars, on 'ships nestling down with their cheeks against the Tramway Centre and sleeping until the bananas are unloaded'. The Centre has never recovered from that loss: it lacks buildings of scale and dignity, and the neatly grassed gardens only underline the need for a strong central feature. Perhaps Bristol should commission some statuary symbolic of its maritime past. But the city council have much bigger questions to ponder. What sort of future do we want for the city docks? There is strong official encouragement for a marina, with floating restaurant, along St. Augustine's Reach. It's a welcome prospect, but the crucial factor in any new schemes, whatever their nature, is how well they are done.

Will Bristol again settle for third best, or will it transform its moribund waterfront into something really exciting? Two splendid warehouse conversions point the way. Ponton and Gough's extraordinary red-brick Bristol 'Byzantine' granary on Welsh Back now reverberates to the sounds of 'Avon Cities' jazz. And on Narrow Quay, a former tea warehouse has been adapted for the Arnolfini contemporary arts complex, with offices on the upper floors. Bush House, a sombre grey pennant stone building dates from 1830 when it was used by merchants Acraman, Bush, Castle & Co. for their tea trade with China. It later served as a granary and a bonded tobacco warehouse.

The Old Granary, now a jazz club

St. Augustine's Reach, looking
towards the Centre, is the site
for the new marina

43

Arnolfini is one of Bristol's outstanding success stories. It was founded by Jeremy Rees as a modest art gallery over a bookshop in The Triangle in 1961 and after several moves has now settled permanently on Narrow Quay. The new complex, completed in 1975, has been described by *The Observer* newspaper as the grandest art centre in the country. Here you can see avante garde exhibitions, buy modern prints, enjoy contemporary music, dance and cinema. There's a good restaurant and well stocked arts bookshop. The atmosphere is relaxed, encouraging open-minded browsing.

- *Fairbairn steam crane dating from 1876*

From Prince Street Bridge is a famous view of St. Mary Redcliffe church, and across the water, on Princes Wharf, is the site for Bristol's planned Museum of Technology, a major boost to the revitalisation of the docks. Nearby, the 35-ton Fairbairn steam crane built by Stothert & Pitt in 1876 has been restored to working condition. It is officially designated as an ancient monument. Thanks to the initiative of City Docks Ventures Ltd., a private company specially formed for the purpose, two more cranes on this wharf have recently been saved. Others, too, will probably now survive.

So there is much to fire the imagination and help shape the future redevelopment of the docks—old warehouses, industrial relics, stretches of cobble, dockside bollards bearing ironfounders' names, lockside cottages, splendid views and, above all, a most remarkable survival. In Charles Hill's shipyard Brunel's great iron ship, s.s. *Great Britain*, patiently undergoes her slow restoration. One hundred thousand people a year file through the turnstiles to marvel at the miracle of her return from the Falkland Islands.

s.s. Great Britain being restored in her original dry dock

Launched on July 19th, 1843, the *Great Britain* was the Great Western Steamship Company's answer to American domination of the transatlantic passenger trade. She was then the largest ship ever built, the first ocean-going vessel to be made of iron and screw propelled. At the time, her dimensions were staggering—322 feet long, almost 3,000 tons and capable of carrying 130 crew and up to 360 passengers. For the best part

of one hundred years the *Great Britain* was a working ship. Much modi-
fied over the years, she plied the Atlantic until 1852, made thirty-two
round voyages from Liverpool to Melbourne (in 1861 carrying the first
All-England cricket eleven to visit Australia), and was later converted to a
cargo sailing ship by Antony Gibbs, Sons & Co. In 1886 storm damage
forced her into the Falklands where she was sold and converted for storage.
Fifty years later, she was written off, towed to Sparrow Cove, beached
and left to break up.

That alone would have been a remarkable history. Her most glorious
episode, though, was yet to come—her homecoming in July, 1970.
Bristolians turned out in their thousands to witness a legend in the making,
as the great ship passed up the Avon, beneath Clifton Suspension Bridge to
return to her original Great Western dry dock. Her rescuers had done the
impossible. The full saga of the rescue operation is racily recounted by
Richard Goold-Adams, chairman of the s.s. *Great Britain* Project in *The
Return of the Great Britain*. He tells a compelling story of the immense
technical, diplomatic and financial hurdles which had to be overcome.

The restoration scheme is to fully restore the exterior appearance of
Brunel's original ship and enough of the interior to illustrate life on a
mid-nineteenth century passenger liner. When it is completed, Bristol
will have yet another great memorial to its remarkable past.

The *Great Britain* was the second of three great ships designed by
Brunel. The first, the *Great Western*, was built as a sort of extension of the
Great Western Railway linking London, through Bristol, with New
York. The Great Western Steamship Company was formed for this
specific project, and the pioneer ship—the first steam ship to be built for
the North Atlantic crossing—was launched from Patterson's Yard in 1837.
A plaque on Princes Wharf commemorates the occasion. Despite its
critics, the 1,340 ton wooden paddle-wheel steamer made her maiden
voyage to New York in fifteen days the following year.

Strangely, Bristol has no statue to Brunel (in a city full of statues,
plaques, busts and effigies) but his greatest monuments, of course, are his
work. He designed, but did not live to see, the Clifton Suspension Bridge.
He was appointed engineer to the Great Western Railway when he was
thirty and designed the company's Temple Meads Terminus. The neo-
Tudor building still stands at the foot of the incline to the present station

and Brunel's superb timber-roofed train shed survives as a British Rail car park. His name is commemorated in Brunel House, in St. George's Road behind the Council House. This was built as The Royal Western Hotel, at Brunel's suggestion, to accommodate passengers transferring from the railway to the *Great Western* steamship. It was a short-lived venture and the building is now used as offices.

The City Docks can be explored on foot, from Mr. Coleman's horse-drawn bus (from Neptune Statue to s.s. *Great Britain*), from Nick and Corinna Gray's *Bristol Packet* narrowboats (still carrying coal on the Grand Union Canal until 1970) or their 1920 riverboat *Tower Belle*, or

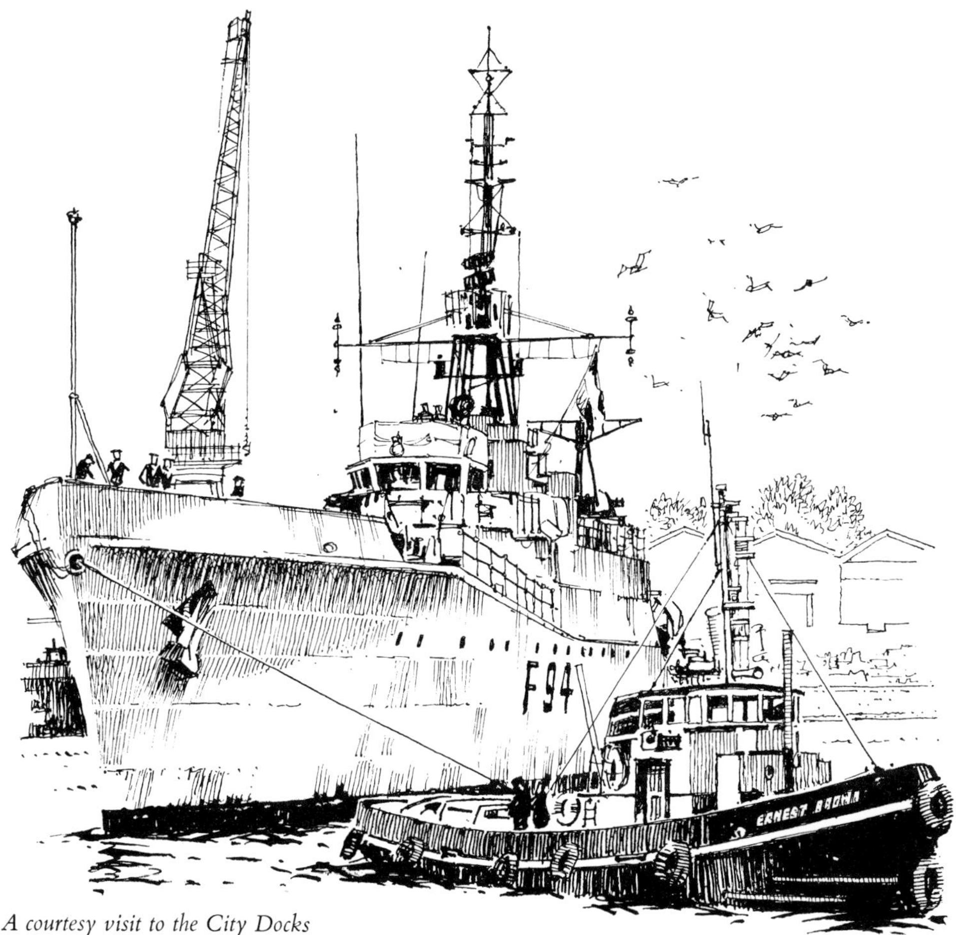

A courtesy visit to the City Docks

from the ferry operated by City Docks Ventures. For the more reflective there are the quayside hostelries. The Nova Scotia, facing the pretty dock cottages at Cumberland Basin and the Ostrich, at the other end of the harbour, near the snad-and-gravel Bathurst Basin with its converted lightship *John Sebastian*, are former sailors' pubs. Keith Brace, in his truly evocative *Portrait of Bristol* summed up the Nova Scotia scene as a little W. W. Jacobs world. It is not a bad description, for Cumberland Basin, despite the noise of the flyover traffic, is a pleasant and interesting spot, especially when there are ships negotiating the lock. Within the Floating Harbour, weekend sailors potter around, watched by young Hotwells families meeting for a lunchtime drink. Nearby, the immense red brick tobacco warehouses are witnesses to one of Bristol's great industries. To the north, Windsor Terrace, where Hannah More once lived, rises sheer from the Avon Gorge and behind, the seemingly light-as-air Clifton Suspension Bridge spans seven hundred feet. Across the bridge, the sheep grazing on Rownham Hill are a pleasing reminder that land is being farmed minutes from the centre of the city.

The Customs House, built in 1836 to replace the one burned down in the Bristol Riots five years earlier

Some Statues & Squares

'MEET NEPTUNE 1.45 sharp.' Neptune's statue at the head of the Floating Harbour has for years been a favourite congregating place for travelling sportsmen. He is the city's best known statue, too. Old guide books mistakenly relate how a grateful citizen of Temple presented the statue in 1588 to commemorate the defeat of the Spanish Armada. This splendid lead figure was, in fact, cast in 1723 for the Temple Conduit and for many years stood in various spots near Temple Church. The inscription records that it was erected on the present spot on May 10th, 1949, latitude 51° 27′ 06″ north, longitude 2° 35′ 47″ west.

Nearby plaques commemorate the voyages of John and Sebastian Cabot, Captain Thomas James' attempt to find the North West Passage and Samuel Plimsoll's efforts on behalf of merchant seamen. Two other famous names are celebrated in The Centre. The great reformer, Edmund Burke, represented Bristol in Parliament from 1774 to 1780, but after a while the West Country merchants found his free thinking, especially on the question of M.P.s' independence, not to their liking. Once elected, Burke rarely visited Bristol, taking the view that he was 'not a member of Bristol but a member of Parliament'. His Bristol election speeches were later described as an epoch in constitutional history, with his laying down for ever the law of the relations between members and constituencies. Burke's statue, a gift of W. H. Wills, was unveiled in 1894 by the Prime

*Neptune's statue at the head of the
Floating Harbour*

Minister, the Earl of Rosebery. It was a replica of a marble statue to Burke in St. Stephen's Hall in the Houses of Parliament.

Near the Cenotaph stands the statue of Bristol's best known benefactor. Born in Temple Street in 1636, Edward Colston became a wealthy merchant. He made most of his fortune in London, but it was his birthplace which received most of his charity—to the tune, probably, of around £100,000, then a truly vast sum of money. His good works are to be seen throughout the city—two schools, the great almshouses on St. Michael's Hill, improvements to the Merchants' Almshouses in King Street, restoration work on the Cathedral and other churches. But his influence extends beyond his personal benefactions, for the charitable societies founded after his death still flourish.

The city's bells tolled for sixteen hours when Colston's body was brought back to Bristol on his death at Mortlake in 1721. He lies in All Saints' Church, City, marked by a statue by Rysbrach. Visitors will see the nosegay of flowers still placed there in his memory every week. Colston's statue on the Centre was erected in 1895. Its designer, John Cassidy, depicted the philanthropist leaning thoughtfully on his staff musing, it has been suggested, on his involvement with the slave trade.

In Queen Square is another example of Rysbrach's work. His depiction of William III on horseback is one of the finest equestrian statues in the country. This is Bristol's greatest square, too. It dates from the early years of the eighteenth century and was for many years a fashionable place to live, its social life at one time centering on the Theatre Royal and the

*In Broadmead, John Wesley's statue outside the
first Methodist chapel in the world*

51

Edward Colston in pensive mood

Assembly Rooms which then stood in nearby Prince Street. The square was laid out on what was formerly The Marsh, an open space outside the original city where Bristolians disported themselves playing bowls and baiting bulls.

Here was the scene of the famous Bristol Riots of 1831 when drunken mobs plundered and burnt down the Mansion House and Customs House and with them all the north and most of the west side of the square. The troubles were sparked by the great Reform issue but also reflected the deep social division of the time. Unrest came to a head when Sir Charles Wetherell, the unpopular Recorder of Bristol, came to open the assizes. Wetherell was a staunch opponent of parliamentary reform, trouble was expected and Government troops were drafted in to help keep the peace. The mere presence of the cavalry seems to have made matters worse. The Recorder succeeded in opening the assizes at the Guildhall and reached the Mansion House in Queen Square, shaken but unharmed, before fleeing the city in disguise. The riots now started in earnest. The Mansion House was looted and destroyed, the Customs House and private houses in Queen Square suffering the same fate; drunken looters roamed the streets, the gaols were burned and their prisoners released, and the Bishop's Palace was destroyed. The riots lasted three days until troop reinforcements finally restored law and order.

William Muller was one of several artists present to record the destruction, but the most vivid account was given by writer Charles Kingsley.

St. Paul's Church, Portland Square

He was then a schoolboy in Bristol and later in life recalled that 'it was an afternoon of sullen, autumn rain. The fog hung thick over the docks and lowlands. Glaring through the fog I saw a bright mass of flame, almost like a half-risen sun. That, I was told, was the gate of the new gaol on fire—that the prisoners had been set free. . . . The fog rolled slowly upward. By ten o'clock that night, one seemed to be looking down upon Dante's Inferno, and to hear the multitudinous moan and wail of lost spirits surging to and fro amid that sea of fire. Right behind Brandon Hill rose the central mass of fire, till the little mound seemed converted into a volcano. . . . Higher and higher the fog was scorched and shrivelled upward by the fierce

Rysbrach's statue of William III, possibly the finest equestrian statue in the country

heat below, glowing through and through with reflected glare till it arched itself into one vast dome of red-hot iron, fit roof for all the madness down below—and beneath it, miles away, I could see the lovely tower of Dundry shining red—the symbol of the old faith, looking down in stately wonder and sorrow upon the fearful birth-throes of a new age.'

An early Queen Square resident was Captain Woodes Rogers whose most popular claim to fame was his friendship with Alexander Selkirk upon whose exploits Defoe based *Robinson Crusoe*. His house was de-molished in 1889 to make way for the florid lines of the Port of Bristol Authority offices. Although fewer than one third of its original buildings have survived, Queen Square remains a handsome show piece. Number 37 housed the second American consulate in Britain and a plaque tells us that Kosciuszko, the Polish patriot, stayed here in 1797. Eça de Queiroz, the great Portuguese writer, was his country's consul at Number 33 from 1878 to 1888. A plaque at Number 38 Stoke Hill records that he lived there during this period and while there wrote part of his *Letters from England*. The new Customs House on the north side of the square is by Sydney Smirke and dates from 1836. Today the square is a fashionable business address, with firms of solicitors, insurance companies, merchant banks and the offices of Bristol's largest advertising agency. The square's appearance would be immensely improved if the cars could be banished from the office forecourts.

For another interesting statue, one might visit the Broadmead shopping area to see John Wesley. Here the great preacher established the New Room, the first Methodist chapel in the world, in 1739. John Wesley came to Bristol that year, in the footsteps of his Oxford friend, George Whitefield, who had preached successfully in the city two years previously. Wesley's first open air meeting attracted an audience of three thousand. He was soon to be debarred from Bristol pulpits, however, on account of his provocative style and was forced to find premises in which his congregations could listen and worship. The New Room, chastely simple, is a haven of peace from the bustle of the Broadmead shops, immensely quiet save for the tick of the eighteenth century clock which was used to time the length of sermons. There is an interesting two-decker pulpit and a German Snetzler organ installed in 1930, although in Wesley's day no musical instruments were used. The box pews, too, are a later addition as the congregation originally sat on benches, the men segregated from the women by a dividing panel down the centre. John Wesley is reputed to have delivered over 40,000 sermons, and travelled a quarter million miles mostly on horseback. So his statue, which dates from 1932, shows him appropriately enough on horseback. In a garden pretty with hydrangea, fuschia and honeysuckle on the Horsefair side stands a statue to brother Charles Wesley, the hymn writer, whose former home at 4 Charles Street, St. James Barton, is marked with a plaque.

The New Room is one of a handful of outstanding buildings which survived the replanning of Bristol's main shopping district. After Hitler's bombs had destroyed the ancient shopping streets around St. Mary-le-port, the planners decided to start afresh. Instead of rebuilding on the old site, they chose to demolish nearby Broadmead, laying down formal thoroughfares and uniform buildings which bore no relation to the huddled intimacy which had endeared the old Mary-le-port area to

Bristolian hearts. Broadmead's severity has been softened by tree planting and pedestrianisation but financial stringency has killed, at least for the present, a number of more ambitious proposals for the area.

The thirteenth century Quakers' Friars, originally a monastery, subsequently used by the Bakers' and Cutlers' guilds, and extended by the Society of Friends in 1747, now houses the Registrar of Births, Deaths and Marriages, and the City's permanent planning exhibition. In nearby Merchant Street are the former Merchant Tailors' Almshouses, dating from 1701, and now a branch of Lloyds Bank. The restoration of this beautiful building won a Civic Trust Award in 1960. Adjoining John Wesley's chapel is the Lower Arcade, running from Broadmead to the Horsefair, a handsome covered way with fluted Ionic columns at either end. It dates from 1824, fortunately surviving the blitz in which the Upper Arcade was lost and adds considerable dignity to its surroundings. In design if not in the quality of its shops, it rivals London's Burlington Arcade. Opposite stands the Greyhound Hotel, an old coaching inn in which the painter W. J. Turner is reckoned to have passed the time of day when visiting friends nearby.

Just north of Broadmead lies Portland Square. Many of its fine houses have been restored and converted into offices, now standing empty awaiting tenants. Its seedy surroundings and curious sense of isolation (the roar of traffic on the nearby inner circuit road notwithstanding) will delay its full rescuscitation, but the day will surely come when a Portland Square address will vie with almost any in Bristol. In the meantime, faded wall advertisements for long departed graphic engravers and miscellaneous commercial undertakings—Number 6 was once 'Head Office, Feather Flake the quality self raising flour'—remind us of the square's chequered history. It started with disaster, victim of the speculative mania which gripped Bristol towards the end of the eighteenth century. When the developers were bankrupted in the great collapse of 1793, the houses were left abandoned, roofless, for years to come. Eventually completed, the square enjoyed a long period of fashion but by the start of the twentieth century, the manufacturers and warehousemen had moved in.

In its heyday, Portland Square had its share of notable residents whose names mean little today. Jane Porter, a highly esteemed writer of her time, died at Number 29 on May 24th, 1850. Her masterpieces were *Thaddeus*

Houses in Canynge Square, Clifton

57

of Warsaw and *The Scottish Chiefs*, which was said to have inspired Sir
Walter Scott to pen his Waverley Novels. E. W. Godwin lived at
Number 21. He had been born at 12 Old Market Street in 1833. Articled
to the City Surveyor he set up his own architectural practice at the age of
twenty-one. In 1862, now married, he moved to Portland Square. Ellen
Terry, as a young actress, played at the Theatre Royal and joined in
Shakespearian readings at the architect's house. Godwin later moved to
London, renewed his friendship with Ellen Terry, by then married
to the artist G. F. Watts, and set up home with her. Architect,
furniture and theatre designer, writer and Orientalist (some of his
furniture designs were in the Japanese idiom), Godwin became a
major figure on the London scene. He designed a Chelsea house for the
artist, Whistler, and Max Beerbohm described him as 'the greatest
Aesthete of them all'.

St. Paul's Church, completed by David Hague in 1794, dominates the
square with its tiered semi-Chinese tower. Purists have deplored its
'rather monstrous' design, but it adds a jolly note to the otherwise
staidish square. It has a fine classical interior. The best view of the church
is across the railed square gardens, its tower framed by the massive
chestnut trees.

Berkeley Square, which one finds at the top of the little street alongside
George's Bookshop, is another Bristol square conceived on the grand
scale, dating from around 1800. Its houses are now converted to office use.
John Addington Symonds, famous in his day for his writings on the
Italian Renaissance, was born at Number 7 on October 5th, 1840. His
local writings included an essay, *Clifton and a Lad's Love*. Better remembered is John Loudon McAdam who lived at Number 23 from 1805 to
1808. He invented the system of roadmaking which bears his name,
became general surveyor to the Bristol Turnpike Trust and set road
standards for the rest of the country.

In the central gardens of Berkeley Square stands a quaint piece of
Bristol history. It is the partially restored replica of the medieval Bristol
Cross. The original cross of 1373 stood in High Street, was moved to
College Green and eventually to Stourhead, now a National Trust
property. A Victorian replica was erected on College Green in 1851, to
be removed a hundred years later when the city council lowered the level

of the green. Discarded by the authorities, the cross was restored by private subscription and moved to its present site in the 1950's.

Bristol is full of interesting squares. In the Clifton suburb, the grand Victoria Square and the tiny Canynge Square remain firmly residential. And it's impossible not to be enchanted by Dowry Square: intimate, pretty and still partly lived in. It lies in Hotwells, at the foot of Hope Chapel Hill, its situation marred only by the swirl of commuter traffic from the Cumberland Basin flyover. Sir Humphrey Davy, of miner's lamp fame, developed laughing gas as an anaesthetic whilst living at Number 6 at which address the Pneumatic Institution was established in 1799. As a boy, the marine painter Wilde Parsons lived at Number 13, where his father ran the Clifton Dispensary. It was said of the artist that no one ever painted the muddy waters of the Bristol Channel so truthfully. He completed many dock scenes, including one massive representation recalling a visit of Queen Elizabeth I to the city and which now hangs in the St. Nicholas Museum.

Foster's Almshouses at the top of Christmas Steps

Christmas Steps

THE PLEASANTLY named Christmas Steps (there are forty-nine of them) are a good place to capture something of the flavour of old Bristol. There was already an ancient footway here when 'steppered done' in 1669 at the personal expense of Jonathan Blackwell, vintner, and the recessed seats near the top of the steps were reputed to have been erected by the inmates of St. Bartholomew's Hospital who sat there seeking alms and selling relics to passers-by.

The shops in Christmas Steps are a curious mixture of the prosaic and the unusual. You can buy buttons galore from Messrs. Trull & Co., tailor's trimmers; mandolins and Brock burglar alarms; secondhand books from Mr. George who still insists on pricing volumes at two-and-sixpence; antiques of all descriptions; Mason's old English extract of dandelion and burdock; rare stamps from Messrs. Urch, Harris & Co.; and rubber noses from Mr. Joe Devotee's novelty shop. At the foot of the Steps connoisseurs reckon you can buy the best fish and chips in Bristol.

Bristol's famous Christmas Steps

-FRANK SHIPSIDES -1977-

Entrance to the medieval St. Bartholomew's Hospital

Next door, is the entrance to the medieval St. Bartholomew's Hospital where the City Museum's department of archaeology has been excavating. Little remains of the earliest buildings but excavations reveal old pillars and other physical evidence to supplement existing documentary information about the early history of the site. It served as a hospital (in the original sense, meaning an almshouse for the sick and the poor) from around 1240 to 1532. It then became the home of Bristol Grammar School until 1767, when it was largely rebuilt and taken over by the pupils of Queen Elizabeth's Hospital until their move to Brandon Hill in the mid-nineteenth century. Since then, the site has seen a variety of commercial uses. St. Bartholomew's is now part of the planned redevelopment around Christmas Steps and Colston Street. There are two schemes—one for each side of the Steps—and the architect's impressions suggest that the mixture of restoration and new building will greatly improve a sadly run down corner of the city. A new building at the foot of the Steps, enclosing the view looking down, will restore the intimacy lost when the east side of Christmas Street was demolished for road widening.

At the top of the Steps are Foster's Almshouses with their strangely named Chapel of the Three Kings of Cologne. The almshouses were founded in 1483 by John Foster, a former mayor, and the chapel in 1504 in honour of God and the three wise men of the East, Melchior, Gasper and Balthazar whose bodies, it was said, found a permanent resting place in the Cathedral of Cologne. The almshouses were rebuilt in 1861 in the Burgundian style, red brick and timber with spiral stairway and ornamental turrets. They are administered by Bristol Municipal Charities.

Behind a plain red door, just a few hundred yards away in Park Row, lies one of Bristol's greatest treasures—the stunning Elizabethan interior of the Red Lodge. The *pièce de résistance* is the superb Great Oak Room, hardly changed in almost four hundred years, with intricately carved panelling, magnificent interior porch, plasterwork and—the crowning feature—an elaborately carved stone chimney piece. There are other fine rooms and marvellous furniture throughout the building. And, like so many good things in Bristol, it's all free.

A handsome seventeenth century stone fireplace in the Savages' wigwam, but formerly in the Goat in Armour Inn on Broad Quay, which may have been the residence of the Master of the Guild of Bakers. The motto on the coat of arms, 'Prais God for all', is used at all Savage functions.

The Red Lodge was built for John Yonge in 1590 as one of two lodges to his Great House where Queen Elizabeth stayed on her visit to Bristol in 1574. The Great House itself housed Colston School before being demolished in 1861 when the school moved to Stapleton. The Colston Hall now occupies the site. The Lodge in the meantime changed hands frequently. From 1827 to 1845 it was the residence of Dr. James Cowles Prichard, an eminent physician and ethnologist who wrote *The Natural History of Man* while living there. In 1854, Mary Carpenter, with financial help from Lady Byron, the poet's widow, opened the first Girls' Reformatory School in the country—'for the restoration to society of girls who have cut themselves off by dishonest practices'—and remained in charge until her death twenty-three years later. The school closed in 1919, and one room is now devoted to a display of the reformer's life and work. In the following year, the Lodge became the home of Bristol Savages, who moved from their old 'Wigwam' at Brandon Cottage. The Savages built a new meeting place in the Red Lodge grounds, and the rest of the building is now open, as part of the City Museum, every afternoon except Sundays.

The Bristol Savages are one of Bristol's most original societies, continuing today the traditions laid down by their founder members, Ernest Ehlers, Arthur Wilde Parsons and others who met weekly as a sketching club from 1894 and formally founded the Society in 1904. The society was originally for artists only, the members meeting weekly to sketch a subject nominated by their chairman for the evening. The two-hour sketch is still the focal point of the tribe's Wednesday evening meet-

The Skinner chair (1660-1690) is one of many treasures in The Red Lodge, and was used by King Edward VII at the opening of the Royal Edward Dock, Avonmouth. The arms are attributed to Robert Skinner, Bishop of Bristol in the seventeenth century.

ings, but over the years it has been supplemented by poetry, monologues, song, piano and instrumental music and good companionship. Anyone lucky enough to spend an evening with the Savages will enjoy a few hours of excellent entertainment. There are about 450 members, divided into three classes: artists, who wear the red feather; blue feather entertainers; and 'lay' members who sport the green. All share the tribe's objective of promoting interest in the arts. Outstanding in the early days was Alderman James Fuller Eberle, chairman of the Art Gallery for some years. It was largely through his efforts that the Society developed so successfully. The artists hold an annual exhibition each Spring, when for two weeks the public may visit the Wigwam and enjoy a representative showing of some of the best paintings in Bristol, as distinct from their weekly two-hour sketches. The tribe has attracted as members many of

St. Michael's Hill, with fine old houses and splendid views

Bristol's leading artists; from the earliest days alone, names like Wilde Parsons, Ernest Board who painted the immense Cabot and 'People who made Bristol great' pictures in St. Nicholas Church Museum, C. Brooke Branwhite who composed masterly sunsets and snow scenes, and the armless painter, Bertram Hiles. As a young lad, Hiles lost both arms in an accident but incredibly trained himself to hold a brush in his teeth. With great courage and determination, he went on to produce really good paintings. His *Sunshine and Shadow* was exhibited at the Royal Academy in 1909 and is now one of the Savages' proudest possessions.

St. Michael's Hill continues the relentless climb through Christmas Steps, up another flight and across seedy Perry Road, towards the Victorian villas of Redland. The run down area at the foot of the hill around St. Michael's church (or St. Michael on the Mount Without, to give its full twelfth century name) has a sombre Dickensian feel. The present church retains an older tower but was otherwise rebuilt by the Paty family in the 1770s. It has a pleasant, homely atmosphere (no bad thing for a place of worship) but architecturally is not especially remarkable. On Easter Tuesday, children are given huge buns, called 'twopenny starvers', continuing a tradition which dates back at least one hundred and fifty years and possibly very much longer. Until quite recently the buns were supplied by four generations of bakers who lived in St. Michael's Hill itself.

The hill has many fine old houses, some of which have recently been restored, and which are well illustrated in *Bristol and how it grew*, Dorothy Brown's excellent study of the city's development from earliest times. This is a fascinating area to explore for the rich variety of its architectural styles and roof-lines, its panoramic views contrasting with sudden tantalising glimpses down gas lit lanes, its raised pavings, steps and iron-work—and all the bits and pieces that give personality to a place. The hill's finest building is Colston's Almshouses, built in 1691 to house twelve men and twelve women and now providing accommodation for four married couples and twelve single persons. Residents sit in the late afternoon sun as their predecessors have through the centuries, and enjoy much the same views.

At Nos. 34-40 St. Michael's Hill lies a thoughtful piece of new building, much more sympathetic to the street scene than other recent additions.

Winstone Court—an attractive group of eleven flats for 'elderly and active' people—was built for the Redland Housing Society and is dedicated to Mr. Reece Winstone 'for his service to Bristol through his pictorial recording of its history'. It is a well deserved tribute, for without Mr. Winstone's remarkable efforts our knowledge of old Bristol would be inestimably poorer. The sheer statistics are overwhelming. Since 1957, with the publication of *Bristol as it was 1939-1914* (note the characteristic reversal of the dates) his various Bristol titles have sold something approaching 150,000 copies. His collection of Bristol photographs, augmented by gifts from many Bristolians, has grown to over 10,000 items. And it all started by accident! Mr. Winstone once explained: 'In 1937 I was a freelance illustrator, a photographer. I took photographs of everything—not just architecture. I calculate that I've had work published in over one thousand different magazines from all over the world. About 1941 I realised I had photographed many of the buildings lost in the blitz, and I began making lantern slides of the negatives. A friend passed on some old photographs of Bristol at the turn of the century which gave me the idea of collecting Victorian views of Bristol, going back as far as possible to when photography was first invented. As people hear of me they send me old photographs instead of throwing them away. They now come in by almost every post. Eventually I had enough lantern slides to make up illustrated talks for sixteen evenings, and people suggested I make up a book of photographs. But none of the London publishers I tried were interested; they said there wasn't enough general interest. It was only the encouragement of a friend, Miss Marguerite Fedden, that persuaded me to take the great step forward and publish them myself.'

Brandon Hill with St. George's Church and Cabot Tower

College Green

AT THE City Museum each year a 'Twenty Ideas for Bristol' exhibition produces a variety of schemes to make the city a pleasanter place in which to live. Anyone with a project to suggest—big or small, simple or grand in conception—is encouraged to participate. There were twenty-eight entries in last year's exhibition, from a community farm to a funicular for Kingsdown. When there is little money to spare, the essence of a good 'idea' lies in its simplicity. This is a virtue of one scheme to enliven College Green with avenues of trees, a box hedge maze, conservatories with birds and butterflies, and an English oak to commemorate the legend that hereabouts St. Augustine of Canterbury sat under his oak to receive the Welsh Bishops nearly fourteen centuries ago. Many Bristolians still remember College Green as a delightful spot, with mature trees and pleasant walks giving it a proper 'Cathedral close' atmosphere. In the 1950s, the green was lowered, the replica High Cross removed and the trees cut down to allow a better view of the new municipal offices. Since then, a few trees have been planted but the new green remains a not quite worthy setting for a great Cathedral and a fine Council House.

Bristol Cathedral with Queen Victoria's statue in the foreground

69

The Abbey gateway, one of Bristol's finest Norman survivals

Except to scholars of church architecture, Bristol Cathedral is perhaps one of Britain's least known cathedrals. And yet it has been described as architecturally one of the most exciting buildings in England. Many of its features were innovations in their time, and Sir Nikolaus Pevsner argues that this was probably the first great 'hall church', with aisles and nave of the same height, in Europe. It was originally the church of the Augustinian abbey founded by Robert FitzHardinge in 1140 and became a cathedral church in 1542 following the dissolution of the monasteries. The Norman survivals, notably the chapter house with its rare arcading, are among the finest to be seen anywhere. A rather stolid exterior gives the layman no clue of the marvels to be found inside. Here, the most exciting elements date from the early fourteenth century—the chancel with aisles and eastern Lady Chapel; but the nave and western towers are the work of G. E. Street, the Victorian architect. Notable among the furnishings is the delicate brass candelabrum dating from 1460 and said to be the oldest and most precious in any English church. It portrays the Virgin and Child and St. George slaying the Dragon.

The Council House, a wide-sweeping neo-Georgian crescent, was started in 1935 but, with the war and economic reconstruction intervening, was not completed until the mid-1950s. Its architect was E. Vincent Harris. The pavilions at either end are surmounted by golden unicorns (from the City's coat of arms) which symbolise reverence towards the

virtuous. At the centre, stands
Sir Charles Wheeler's sculpture
of an Elizabethan sailor, over-
looking a rather tame stretch of
water with fountains. Inside, the
Council Chamber has a marvellous ceiling by John Armstrong,
a sort of Bristol fantasy of ships,
buildings and allegorical figures.
In the Conference Room is Sir
Tom Monnington's immense
geometrical abstract painting in
tempera. It is one of the largest
painted ceilings in the country.
But visitors on the tours
arranged by the City Public
Relations Department will find
much more to interest them,
especially perhaps the walnut-
panelled Lord Mayor's Parlour
with its marvellous civic in-
signia, much of which is still
used for city ceremonial.

Tucked in between the row
of shops on College Green, its
red sandstone tower almost
hidden from view, is St. Mark's,

One of the Council House pavilions surmounted by a golden unicorn

better known as the Lord Mayor's Chapel. This is said to be the only
municipally owned chapel in the country. It dates from 1230 and is all
that remains of the medieval Gaunt's Hospital. At the Dissolution,
Henry VIII sold the chapel to Bristol Corporation for £1,000, the French
Huguenots used it from 1687 to 1722 after which it became the Corporation's official place of worship. The chapel thus plays an important part
in the city's ceremonial life. Inside is a treasure house of beautful things—
the sixteenth century French and Flemish stained glass, William Edney's
magnificent wrought iron sword rest, a profusion of monuments to the

Hospital's founders and to city notables. The Poyntz Chapel is noted for its beautifully fan vaulted roof and its sixteenth century Spanish floor tiles.

From College Green rise the shops of Park Street. This was once the West's most fashionable shopping area, when there was a distinct *cachet* about a Park Street address. Although it no longer aspires to that sort of reputation, it is an interesting street with some good shops and one of the best Indian restaurants outside London. Park Street started out in life as a high class residential area in the great eighteenth century building boom. One of Bristol's best known literary figures, Hannah More helped her sisters run a

The Lord Mayor's chapel

fashionable girls' school here from 1767 to 1790. Hannah More's writings are scarcely read today (scholars puzzle at the remarkable success of her novel, *Coelebs in search of a wife*), but she played an important role as philanthropist, moralist and a leader of the intellectual life of the city. The Park Street house was for years the meeting place for local and visiting literati. But none of the acquaintances struck up there could match, for longer term significance, one that took place in 1795 at Number 7 Great George Street. For William Wordsworth's introduction to Samuel Coleridge gave an impetus to the Romantic Movement which transformed English poetry around the turn of the century. The poets' brief links with the city (Coleridge's are the stronger, as he lived here at several addresses) are the high spot of Bristol's literary associations. In 1798, Joseph Cottle produced their *Lyrical Ballads* from his High Street address. Coleridge's contribution included *The Ancient Mariner* and Wordsworth is reputed to have been putting the finishing touches to

Park Street and the University Tower

Tintern Abbey as he strolled down Park Street to complete the manuscript in Cottle's parlour. The Great George Street house, now known as the Georgian House, was built for John Pinney, a wealthy sugar merchant in 1789. It is owned by the city and has been elegantly furnished in a style suitable to the period and to the merchant classes who were commissioning such houses at the time. The house made an ideal setting for the BBC Play of the Month production, in November 1976, of *London Assurance*, Boucicault's stylish comedy of manners.

Dominating the Park Street skyline is the magnificent University Tower, a 215 foot high, richly decorated Gothic masterpiece completed in 1925. Many visitors think it is much older. The tower and surrounding buildings make up the Wills Memorial Building, a gift to the University by George Alfred Wills and Henry Herbert Wills as a memorial to their father who had virtually founded the modern university. Bristol had a university college, dating from 1876, when Henry Overton Wills offered £100,000 (then a truly immense sum) to establish a University provided a charter was obtained within two years. The charter was granted in 1909 and H. O. Wills became the University's first chancellor. The tower was designed by Sir George Oatley, one of Bristol's great architects, and built with meticulous craftsmanship. A fan vaulted vestibule rises 72 feet and a splendid double flight of stone steps leads to the Great Hall with a famous hammer-beam roof and linen-fold panelling. The tower houses the $9\frac{1}{2}$ ton bell which Bristolians quickly dubbed 'Great George', neatly commemorating the triple association of King George V who performed the opening ceremony on June 9th, 1925, Sir George Oatley the architect and Sir George Wills, one of the two benefactors. The Wills tobacco family's remarkable generosity did not stop at this. They have financed other university buildings and halls of residence, purchased the Victoria Rooms for the university students, helped finance the restoration of the Great Hall after war damage and have given liberally for other educational and charitable works.

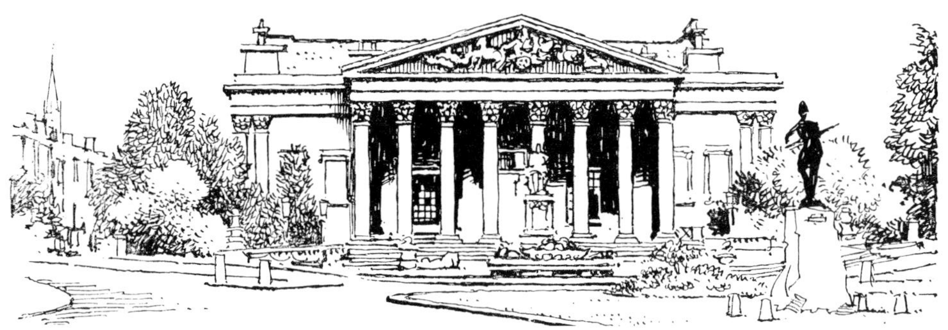

The Victoria Rooms, a popular meeting place and landmark since the 1840s

Clifton

CLIFTON MEANS different things to different people. To visitors, it's crossing the world famous suspension bridge, visiting Bristol Zoo,

Royal York Crescent, once Clifton's most fashionable address

giggling at the camera obscura and walking on the Downs. Or it's browsing around the antiques and bric-à-brac in The Mall. To the literary minded, it's the minor writers commemorated on house plaques and whom nobody reads any more. To estate agents, it's a much-sought-after area with luxury flat conversions and period houses coming back into fashion for family use.

To the student of architecture, Clifton has few outstanding individual buildings, but many crescents, squares and terraces. Royal York Crescent, in Sir John Betjeman's phrase, is a splendid example of spec building on the grand scale. William Lockier, a property promoter, started the

Crescent in 1791, was bankrupted by 1793 and ruined several builders working on the scheme. The partially completed Crescent narrowly escaped being converted into Army barracks, work continued intermittently and the grand design was not finished until 1820. This is Clifton's finest set piece, with its raised terrace where the fashionable used to promenade in the heyday of Clifton society. The houses here are truly immense, each originally with its great drawing room on the first floor measuring 23 feet wide, 28 feet deep and 13 feet high.

Clifton is also the new Roman Catholic Cathedral, not to everyone's taste but winning two major architectural awards, a famous boys' public school, the Lord Mayor's official residence, the Students' Union, leafy walks on quiet Sunday mornings, and marvellous views towards Dundry Hill. It's a relaxed, free wheeling atmosphere, late night parties in the flat above, and a lunchtime drink in the pub or wine bar round the corner.

But above all, to most Bristolians, Clifton means an outing to the Zoo. Each year, there are about three-quarters of a million visitors and on one Whit Monday a record 35,000 people wandered through the twelve acres marvelling at the 1,500 creatures and their beautiful surroundings.

Bristol Zoo, a firm favourite for family outings

It is the fifth oldest zoo in the world and open to the public longer than any other zoo in the United Kingdom. The zoo was founded in 1834, when 225 Bristolians subscribed £25 a share to form the Bristol, Clifton and West of England Zoological Society. Over the years, this has been home to many well known favourites. Older generations remember Alfred, the famous gorilla who lived here from 1930 until he died in 1948, and more recently Dotty, the ring-tailed lemur from Madagascar, has achieved national fame in the *Animal*

The Mall, Clifton with
Francis Greenway's Assembly
Rooms, now **The Clifton Club**

Clifton Suspension Bridge seen from Cumberland Basin

Magic television programmes. The zoo has a highly successful breeding record, and its remarkable white tigers are the only ones in captivity outside India and America.

Clifton's other great tourist attraction, its suspension bridge, had its origin over 200 years ago in a strange bequest by a Bristol wine merchant. In 1754, William Vick left £1,000 to be invested until, with interest, it had accumulated to the £10,000 which he believed would be enough to finance a bridge to span the Avon Gorge between Clifton and Leigh Woods. Little happened until the 1790s when the growth of fashionable Clifton revived interest in the idea. William Bridges then produced a fantastic plan for a bridge and miniature village with houses, shops, corn exchange, chapel and offices beneath the proposed roadway spanning the massive structure. It was totally impracticable and the financial crisis brought on by the war with France killed the idea.

Forty years later, after two competitions, much indecision and acrimony, a scheme by Isambard Kingdom Brunel was accepted. There was an abortive start and further financial difficulties, but work began in earnest in 1836. The sponsors ran out of cash after seven years—£30,000 short of their £75,000 target and the bridge was abandoned. In 1860, by which time Brunel was dead, a further effort was made to complete the project. A new parliamentary act gave the necessary powers, the funds were raised and only four years later more than 100,000 people were turning out to witness the grand ceremonial opening of the great bridge on Thursday, December 8th, 1864—110 years after William Vick's initiative and a fitting tribute to the genius of its designer. The bridge has a total span between piers of 703 feet, stands 245 feet above high water and weighs 1,500 tons.

There have been many anecdotes about the bridge, and Sarah Ann Henley's story is too well known not to be repeated. In 1885, she threw herself off the bridge after a lovers' tiff and, to her great amazement, was gently parachuted by her petticoats into the mud below. She then lived to a grand old age. Aeroplanes have flown under the bridge—the first, in 1911, was piloted by a M. Tetard and the second a year later by Sir Alan Cobham. In 1957, a Royal Air Force pilot lost his life when his Vampire jet aircraft crashed attempting the hazardous feat at 450 miles an hour.

The observatory on the hill above the bridge is all that remains of an old snuff mill which was partly burned down two hundred years ago. In 1828, William West rented the mill and installed a camera obscura. These instruments of innocent *voyeurism* were all the rage before the days of cinema. A mirror in the roof reflects the panorama outside the tower downwards onto a shallow horizontal saucer screen. The operator rotates the mirror so that the audience has an all-round view. The Clifton camera has enthralled Bristolians for years. Its charm was well described by H. V. Morton as 'the illusion it imparts of ominipotence. The people who stroll calmly across the mysterious Merlin's table in the darkened room are deliciously unconscious that the hill has its eye on them. They are so natural that one childishly follows them with a finger and pinches the empty air in a futile attempt to pick them up.'

If one stands on the steps of the Victoria Rooms, the imposing building on the left next to Debenhams belongs to the Royal West of England Academy. It dates from the middle of the last century, but in 1911 the outer flights of steps were removed and, inside, a splendid marble staircase was built, leading to an upper foyer with four large murals by Walter Crane.

Looking from Boyces Avenue into Victoria Square

The Academy owes its existence to the generosity of Mrs. Ellen Sharples, an amateur artist whose husband was a well known pastel portrait artist and whose daughter, Rolinda, is remembered today for her intriguing scenes of Bristol social life in the early nineteenth century. Ellen Sharples was seventy-five, and her husband and daughter both dead, when in 1844 she provided the Bristol Society of Artists with the funds to found an Academy of Art. Four years later she bequeathed her whole estate including a valuable collection of pictures. A

*The Royal West of England Academy contrasts nicely with
the classical lines of the nearby Victoria Rooms*

merger with the Art Union in 1858 led to the formation of The Bristol Fine Arts Academy which moved into the new building in the same year. The Academy was granted a Royal Charter by King George V in 1913 and its present title dates from that year.

From its early days, the Academy provided tuition for art students, and although it no longer runs art classes itself, its studios are used by Bristol Polytechnic and Brunel University. Between the wars the Academy joined with the Bristol & Somerset Society of Architects to found a successful School of Architecture which was later integrated into the University of Bristol.

The RWA has one of the finest suites of exhibition galleries in the country. About 2,000 works ranging from pencil drawings to life-sized sculptures are submitted to its Open Exhibition each Autumn, of which 600 or so are chosen for hanging. The exhibition attracts about 5,000 visitors. The Academy's other main exhibition, in the Spring, is limited to members' work and the current trend is for group shows. There is also a permanent collection of contemporary paintings and sculptures by members totalling something over 600 items and growing all the time. The collection was started just after the second war, helped enormously by a legacy from Mrs. Augusta Talboys who was herself a member. Selections from the permanent collection are shown at least once a year.

The Academy has about 550 members—artists and associates—including 150 new members who have joined in the last three years, and is seeking to broaden its appeal without prejudicing its main purpose in life. The Council, with Mr. Donald Milner as President, sees its task as 'helping the interests of practising painters and sculptors who are competent and sincere, however different in outlook' and believes it has an especial duty to young and promising artists. A significant departure, in 1977, was a South West Arts exhibition of work by Terry Frost—a well-attended show which pointed the way to further links with the Arts Council and South West Arts.

For further reading

Kathleen Barker: *Bristol at Play*
Geoffrey Body: *Clifton Suspension Bridge*
Keith Brace: *Portrait of Bristol*
Dorothy Brown: *Bristol and how it grew*
T. H. B. Burrough: *Bristol: City Buildings Series*
Clare Crick: *Victorian Buildings in Bristol*
C. F. W. Dening: *The Eighteenth century architecture of Bristol*
C. F. W. Dening: *Old Inns of Bristol*
Tudor Edwards: *Bristol*
Jennifer Gill: *The Bristol Scene*
R. Goold-Adams: *The Return of the s.s. Great Britain*
S. Hutton: *Bristol and its famous associations*
W. Ison: *The Georgian Buildings of Bristol*
J. Latimer: *The Annals of Bristol*
Bryan Little: *The City and County of Bristol*
Patrick McGrath: *The Merchant Venturers of Bristol*
C. M. MacInnes and W. F. Whittard (eds): *Bristol and its Adjoining Counties*
H. V. Morton: *In Search of England*
Nikolaus Pevsner: *North Somerset and Bristol*
J. Sansom and others: *Modern Buildings in Bristol*
Brian Smith and Elizabeth Ralph: *A History of Bristol and Gloucestershire*
Audrey Williamson and Charles Landstone: *The Bristol Old Vic*
Reece Winstone: *Bristol series of photographs*